Read All About Whales

WATCHING WHALES

Jason Cooper

The Rourke Corporation, Inc.
Vero Beach, Florida 32964

© 1996 The Rourke Corporation, Inc.

All rights reserved. No part of this book may be reproduced or utilized in any form or by any means, electronic or mechanical including photocopying, recording or by any information storage and retrieval system without permission in writing from the publisher.

PHOTO CREDITS
©Tom Kitchin: cover, p.19; ©Peter C. Howorth: p.18; ©Mark Conlin/INNERSPACE VISIONS: p.4; ©Brandon Cole: p.6, 12; ©Sea World of Florida, All rights reserved: p.7, 20; ©Frank Balthis: p.9, 13; ©Lynn M. Stone: p.10, 15; ©Marty Snyderman: p.16, 22

Library of Congress Cataloging-in-Publication Data

Cooper, Jason, 1942-
   Watching whales / by Jason Cooper
      p. cm. — (Read all about whales)
   Includes index.
   Summary: Describes how people watch whales and what they learn about their behavior.
   ISBN 0-86593-451-7
   1. Whale watching—Juvenile literature. 2. Whales—Juvenile literature. [1. Whale watching. 2. Whales.]
I. Title II. Series: Cooper, Jason, 1942-   Read all about whales
QL737.C4C65 1996
599.5—dc20
                                            96-19192
                                                  CIP
                                                    AC

Printed in the USA

TABLE OF CONTENTS

Watching Whales 5

Leaping Whales 6

Spy Hopping 8

"Thar She Blows!" 11

Bubble Nets 12

Dive! 14

Swimming with Whales 17

Whales and Kayaks 18

Captive Whales .20

Glossary 23

Index 24

WATCHING WHALES

Imagine being so close to a wild whale that you can smell its fishy breath. On a whale watching boat you can!

Whales are air-breathing **mammals** (MAM uhlz), like us. They must rise to the ocean surface to breathe.

Whale watchers see the whales break through the ocean surface. Sometimes the great whales are just a few feet away.

Several seaside towns in Canada, the United States, and Mexico offer whale-watching trips.

Whale watchers are close enough to this gray whale to feel the mist from its spout.

LEAPING WHALES

Whale watchers enjoy watching the behavior of whales. One of the most exciting sights is a **breach** (BREECH). A breach is a mighty leap.

A leap begins when a whale suddenly lunges from the sea, as if it were trying to jump over the moon.

Lucky whale watchers may see a whale leap from the sea in what is called a breach.

Trained killer whales breach in front of a whale-watching crowd at Sea World in Orlando, Florida.

Scientists aren't sure why whales breach from time to time. Whatever the reason, these leaps by killer, humpback, gray, and other whales are among the greatest shows on Earth.

SPY HOPPING

Whale watching is like reading a good mystery book. You don't know what is going to happen next.

Sometimes whales act shy towards boats. Sometimes whales are very curious. Certain whales even poke their heads out of water for a closer look.

This is called spy hopping. Humpback, killer, and gray whales commonly spy hop.

Whales do not have good vision. By spy hopping, though, they do their best human watching.

A gray whale spy hops for a better look at the whale watchers nearby.

"THAR SHE BLOWS!"

Long ago, a whaler who spied a whale would yell, "Thar she blows!"

What the sailor saw was the whale's blow, or spout, a cloud of water droplets. The whale makes a blow when it breathes out through its blowhole. The blowhole, on top of the whale's head, is its nose. A whale also breathes in through the blowhole.

A sharp-eyed whale watcher can tell the **species** (SPEE sheez), or kind, of whale by the shape of its blow.

These whales are close, but spouts help whale watchers find whales even when they are more than a mile away.

BUBBLE NETS

Whale watchers following humpback whales may see bubbles on a smooth sea. The humpbacks who made the bubbles are below, out of sight. They wait while little fish called herring gather inside the bubble "net," which is really a ring of bubbles.

Feeding humpbacks gulp herring after surrounding the little fish with a "net" of bubbles.

A "friendly" gray whale surfaces to the delight of whale watchers at Laguna San Ignacio, Mexico.

Herring aren't really trapped by the bubbles, but they think they are. Moments after the bubbles rise, the **pod** (PAHD), or group, of whales lunges into the herring. Humpbacks take in huge mouthfuls of water and little fish.

Humpbacks have comblike **baleen** (buh LEEN) in their jaws. Bristles on the edges of the baleen trap food.

DIVE!

Big whales generally swim slowly along the ocean surface. They feed on small fish and tiny, floating creatures called **plankton** (PLANK ton). A whale, however, may suddenly dive.

Whale watchers often see whales dive. The whale rolls forward and downward. Its tail rises straight up from the sea, like a Y-shaped flag. Then the broad tail rapidly slips beneath the waves.

Whales hunt at different depths of the sea, so some dive deeper than others. The sperm whale can dive more than a mile down!

As if waving goodbye with its tail, a whale rolls and heads down, down, down.

SWIMMING WITH WHALES

Watching whales face to face in their undersea world is a special thrill for **snorkelers** (SNOR kel erz). Snorkelers wear diving masks and a breathing tube, or snorkel.

Whales in the company of snorkelers are usually gentle and shy. Sometimes they're curious.

Marty Snyderman, an underwater photographer, tells of snorkeling with humpback whales. The whales swam just inches away from his mask. "It was incredible," Mr. Snyderman said, "to watch animals so large be so graceful." The whales never bumped the snorkeler.

For a few moments, a snorkeler becomes part of a pod of spotted dolphins.

WHALES AND KAYAKS

In the famous story of Moby Dick, a great white sperm whale attacked a wooden sailing ship. In real life, whales usually avoid bumping ships or even smaller craft. Whale watchers in small boats, like kayaks, feel fairly safe. They wear life jackets, however.

A humpback whale dives while a kayaker appears not to notice.

A pod of killer whales parades past kayaks along the coast of British Columbia, Canada.

Kayakers along the coasts of Alaska and British Columbia paddle along with pods of killer whales.

The kayakers watch the whales spout, breach, dive, and chase schools of salmon. The whales generally ignore the kayakers.

CAPTIVE WHALES

Back on land, whale watchers find whales at some zoos, public aquariums, and entertainment parks. Most captive whales are **belugas** (buh LOO guhz), bottle-nosed dolphins, and killer whales.

Captive whales are rarely longer than 25 feet. Even the largest glass tanks aren't big enough for the super-sized baleen whales.

Captive whales learn certain tasks quickly. Some are trained to leap, play with balls, and dive for objects.

A trainer at Sea World works with a pair of killer whales.

GLOSSARY

baleen (buh LEEN) — the tough, comblike plates found in the upper jaws of certain whales; whalebone

belugas (buh LOO guhz) — small, white whales of Arctic seas

breach (BREECH) — the leap of a whale out of the sea

mammals (MAM uhlz) — the group of air-breathing, warm-blooded, milk producing animals

plankton (PLANK ton) — tiny, floating plants and animals of the sea and other bodies of water

pod (PAHD) — a group of whales, porpoises, or dolphins

snorkeler (SNOR kel er) — one who wears a glass-fronted mask and breathing tube to look underwater while swimming

species (SPEE sheez) — within a group of closely related animals, one certain kind, such as a *blue* whale

Whale watching is always exciting, especially for a diver swimming with giant right whales.

INDEX

aquariums   20
baleen   13
blow   11
blowhole   11
boats   8
breach   6
dolphin, bottle-nosed   20
kayakers   19
kayaks   18
mammals   5
plankton   14
snorkelers   17
Snyderman, Marty   17

spy hopping   8
whale watchers   5, 6
whale watching   5, 8
whales   5, 6, 7, 8, 12, 14, 17, 18, 20
   belugas   20
   gray   7, 8
   humpback   7, 8, 13, 17
   killer   7, 8, 20
   sperm   14, 18
   tail of   14
zoos   20